ATROPHY OF THE BOY WHO BECAME A WISHING WELL

ATROPHY OF THE BOY WHO BECAME A WISHING WELL

∞

Poems

Nathaniel Bek

New York

Copyright © 2021 Nathaniel Bek
All rights reserved.

No part of this book may be reproduced or transmitted in any form or by any means, electronic or mechanical including photocopy, recording or any information storage or retrieval system without prior written permission from the publisher, except for brief quotations used for reviews, scholarly papers or publications.

Three Mile Harbor Press
PO Box 1
Stuyvesant, New York 12173
www.3mileharborpress.com

ISBN: 9780998340654

Library of Congress Control Number: 2021937559

First Edition
Printed in the United States of America

Cover painting by Marc Chagall
Cover design by Pamela Hughes
© All Rights Reserved

Störrisch 9
Colt and the Bit That Lead It 10
Well Water 12
The Boy the Blade the Word 13
The Barn That Held the California Sunset 15
Moving On 16
Where the Glaciers Went When We Were Born 17
Germination 18
The Sun Setting the First Time 24
Testimony of the Sun 25
When a Gun Begins to Be a Gun 27
Roadkill and Other Myths 28
Make a Meal of the Soft 30
Daydream Me a Toto 31
What Is a Cracked Coffee Cup Supposed to Hold 32
The Last Cry of the Buffalo 33
When the Face Is Too Much to Wear 34
Air 36
Hair Caught in the Drain 38
A Whistle in the Tub Drums 39
Body of Water 40
Icarus's Great Hello 43
The Night Barks Back 44
I Drink the Milk Because It Is Whole 45
Fishbowl 47
The Boy/The Bottle/The Erasure 48
There Are No Footsteps in the Deep End 49
Sap and Saplings 51
Sans 53
Thesis on the Feeling of Wings 54
A Good Day's Work 55
A Millionaire / A Taxi Driver / A Tax Paid 57

The Pocket Knife that Learned to Whittle Flutes   59
Cleaned   61
Discovery   63
The Illness that We Breed   64
The Night Is Made of Laughter   65
Gingerbread   66
Asphyxiation of Pain   67
Needles   69
Truth Is a Ghost of Our Speech   70
Lucid   72
Ode to the Man I am Today   73
Dare to Be   74

This book is dedicated to all those who were stubborn enough to stay, and all others we wish had never left.

STÖRRISCH

My art teacher once said
"The clay is as it was born"

And I think of my mother
Her spine cradled me into this
I accepted welcoming like a common burdock
Face full of straw burs
I was born sunny side up, hard against the back
To this day she has never broken
The silence of how she has labored me

And I am as the seed is to earth
A restless palm reaching for the air
A broken shell of a good living
A stubborn massing of roots
Or that of my mother's will
A happening anthology of chances
That finally stayed

My mother tells me of a sister never born
And I am born again
A bundle of lashes, hair, and smiles
Twenty-four hours of unrest wrapping a father's finger
I was unbending enough to arrive
Here like an unfurled bow
A present that has been asked for again
But what open lung has not asked for the same

Is this what keeps me, or

Am I too afraid to return
To everything I have ever called home
Leaving and returning can sound the same
I too am the clay as it was born
A thing of the earth too estranged to stay here

COLT AND THE BIT THAT LEAD IT

I have lost the garden I planted here
Riding that old Little Tikes tractor
Plowing the dust off the soil like
Time was a product of laughter

In the beginning
I chased the shadows of tall tales
Where a man's bare hands were
As good as his word

I saw my father as he saw his

Power is no more a word as it is an experience
And I have seen the way earth was
Moved by those hands
Enough times to know some tales are true

He, my father, held a grown horse
In his arms

Have you ever seen the way domestication
Can shake the nature out of something
I have seen the way 900 lbs. can have the
Open pastures carved out of them

Most things I would imagine
Feel like clay to God
The way anything can be molded so easily
To resemble an idea

The way my father
Was the carpenter, the mason, and
The man

A farmer's son
Broke the earth open enough times
He learned he could make it his own
I wonder if he had a green tractor too

Rodeo'd through the tall grass pastures
Felt the hum of the plastic
Foot pedals and three wheels of madness
A kid can look like anything with a full smile

***

You know the dust always breathes cleaner up here
That's why we never speak of it settling
The earth just one day formed
But we keep dredging it up like there
Is still something to fix

Like the garden we planted off somewhere behind the evergreens
I still look for the smell of soil
The way it clings to your hands
As it did my father's

I wish this could be a metaphor for finding happiness
But in the Midwest, we watch the seasons change too quickly
And nothing ever grows here for long

WELL WATER

The faucet always smelled of garden rake
Pulling through our taste buds like mud
The barn door always said things like
    "You fucking get back in here"
      And I think it was the winter shivering hinges
       That still makes it tough to open up sometimes
        Some things get stuck closed for a reason
The shovel always dug the ground wrong
Set the earth crooked like a cattail in the fall
And the toolshed always held my hands with a hammer like
    "You are going to fucking sit here till you fix it"
      But a child's understanding is a hard thing to nail down
       Calluses and burns make a tough skin
        And so did you
The paint always chipped after a good season
Shed the snow and everything with it
But we coated the wood to hide the rot
    "I'm Sorry"
      Words can be a tree root to a concrete wall
       The way sickness can be of blood
       And bank accounts

    The day we lost everything I met you
  Shook hands with the earth and laid a promise beside the pear trees
      Apologies are not always said
       But act out just the same
       We are all just well water
       Here to return here again
   And I wish for the storm that finally takes this house
   And I speak into the wood and ask it for forgiveness
        I let you in
      But what hello has not stirred this
        Before

THE BOY THE BLADE THE WORD

Back when the world was still as young as I was, and the clouds still spoke in riddles
We would lay in the grass feeling the wind cut comfort into our skin
Go down to the creek and watch as tadpoles became frogs
Became legs
Raw meat for the sharp things that hunger in the bush
Back when we were still boys
Pretending to be children
And manhood hadn't snuck up under our beds like a closed fist after a hard day's work
We were still able to make anything with our hands
Catch butterflies fluttering
Chase dandelions in the wind

Back before the storms came and claimed us numbered
Made arks of our bodies
For our feelings to weather the storm

Cause man don't break tears and silence
Does he

Like skin
Like man
Bottle them up like burning fireflies
There is no night here
To be afraid of
Because what hasn't fear
Already taught you

Boy!

No need for dandelions to wish on
Just be a man
A sharp thing of meat
That cuts the comfort out of you
Out of your skin
Till you are no longer a tadpole
A boy
A thing that still speaks in riddles
When the world was still young

                                            The boy
                                            The blade
                                            The word

                              The stone that named them sharp
                                            The fist
                              All the tools in the shed
                                            A Purpose
Or the shard of the old hammer that had rusted and splintered from so much
work
Stuck so deep his hand amputated all
The speech and the boy was left speechless

                              Remove the meat and let the blood
                              The words and all from the body
                                            The tender
                                            The tender
                              The tender steak beat and raw
                              Eat the tendons and watch the fill
                                  All the connected tissue
                  The man
                       The boy
                              The stone
                                   The fist
                                            The blade
                                            The blade

The sharp they named of all this flesh
And the flesh of all this made sharp
They named it
          They named it
Man

THE BARN THAT HELD THE CALIFORNIA SUNSET

A storm rustled up the remains in these palms / spoke little whispers like fireflies / have you heard the big city streets that make traffic jams of our words / every time we tried to hold on to a thing other than ourselves

I am no longer sure this is about me / but when has anything really been about me-

        Stare out a window long enough and you will find yourself
Maybe not here / but when has here ever been what you are really looking for / I know now who you were / before responsibility claimed you like a gunshot wound

I suppose the world feels like a trip to a child's bedroom sometimes.

I still wear clothes from places I have never been / chew the sunlight as it sets and question if my name means anything / I speak like this skin knows more than my body

        Let the ground name us home
        Make a field of corn to hide our growth in
        Clean the body of the feed
        May we walk this like the horses
        Till we find the cold
        Till we no longer know where we are from

I remember the last time on the farm / head bent to the tired / It was family / that first called me / it was family / that first moved me away / we want to be a part of something but nothing at all

    I wonder

    if

I will return to the country roads / raise young in the silence of the hills
    I wonder if this is what brought you back

                                            The Silence.
                        I wonder if it is what brings us all back.

To where we began.

MOVING ON

"I have dug an organ from under the basement"– Irina Bogomolova, "They Will Not Bleed for Us"

Dad,

>The stains don't wash off the way they used to
>But a tremble in my hand still shakes the water free
>I don't think I will ever find an apology down here
>Just old containers filled with a person I barely knew
>Unboxing this can feel like clemency if I let it
>But where do we put the body when we're done

WHERE THE GLACIERS WENT WHEN WE WERE BORN

One summer I chased the seasons into
The foothills of the North
Rattled the screen door of my friend's
Cabin loud enough it stayed on my hands
Found fear chasing the sun down the street

The gravel
Only took what it had to

At night the moths would make
Cocoons of the walls
We were boys just long enough to
See the leaves fall from the trees

You don't always get to decide how you
Grow up
You don't always get to leave the stovetop burning
Long enough
To pick the garden clean

I am not so sure we ever learn what
It is to be

We are all just lost in the lakes looking
For our father's reflection
And pretending
We know what it looks like

GERMINATION

I

When the world finally stopped and lifted its hands to shake time with the beginning, we were all ants in a burning fire, roasting a raindrop from our lungs. We became whole in flesh, a new meaning made of spare bones. Back when the sun spoke for six days, we kneaded the stones out of birch trees till the blood ran with the children and made roots of the apples while we spoke with snakes. Back when the wood made homes of our bodies and we asked the caves to make artwork of our names. We chanted three times into the stars to return and the silent night came and tucked us in to bed.

II

My mother would make maple syrup of my back the nights she would sing me lullabies and ask for forgiveness. Back then, before oil varnish licked the clean from my hands, I still had feet that faced the way I was talking. I still made a breakfast of smiles and picked joy from my cheeks like kisses.
I was just a boy then, made of grass and soil stains that hadn't learned how to say my name yet. Back then before my body knew the taste of fruit, every hug was like home cooked pancakes and biscuits we could sink our arms into. Kisses were nothing but a stamp on every letter that said I love you.

III

There are days I wish I never found what flesh was for

The earliest memory I have; I don't remember how many birthday candles made molten wax offerings to my cake that year. Disney movies were still made of film and plastic. Spun out and tracked across white static. It was definitely before 1st grade. Before my boyish heart learned what girls could do to it.

I remember reaching for *Hercules* or *The Little Mermaid*. VHS tapes would flicker and crackle as the machine ate the tape into the belly of the screen.

My eyes fused to the hypnotic palpitations of the living picture box

A woman screams, or cries, or lets out a deep moan that sits even deeper in my stomach. Porn and murder can look and sound the same to a young boy. It can caw out the dark and curl the spine into waking. There is a cherry that breaks like a boy's skin and all the juice layers my hands full.

I run

IV

Images and memories can remake themselves in art
Creep out the mouth like gangling fingers

We are all Polaroids in the past

2nd Grade
       Art class
The body makes an appearance
All the applause is held to the end
Nudity is a parent teacher conference or
An office
       An art gallery
Female draped over parchment in a loose jaw of my mother's speech

I hold up my hands like my father speaks
I hide the words in graphite
A slacking babble that I cannot understand
What are hands if not dirty
But it discovers itself in my chest like:

Breasts make milk and strong bones of the wicked

V

We score the banister of my life and twelve chimes of the clock answer
Indiana Jones and Star Wars
Every child adventures into the unknown

I find my father's collection in boxes. Four or five in total, maybe more. I never counted.
Some days I wish I would have found comic books, so I could call them graphic novels.
But graphic doesn't blister the body and leave it vulnerable like this
I learned hair is not just for the head
Beasts make good work of our bodies
When the good aren't wanting

VI

Thirteen years and a child sacrificed to the teens
The boy stays and I hear him in the cold
When my arms ache to the sounds of my haunting
Some secrets hide in plain sight, others make themselves a web

And I have been caught up ever since

Does the computer know we watch it in the night
Make its body and ask it not to speak
Not to look when we make love to ourselves
We are a selfish mass

I have learned to hate my hands and all they have become in the night

I was a child once

Back when my ghost was still a young haunting that leveled my hands raw
and all the years gulped down my boyish charm
The keys gargled out a symphony while I tried to collect myself before the floor

VII

When my brother tells me, he cured the bad box of all its wanting
Removed the digital flesh that bred with our bodies
We learned that the addicts become restless before the dawn

The father will demand a sacrifice
He will ask of you so much more than you can offer
He will ask the boy to fix the box

The boy sits in silence
He doesn't understand how to put the plastic back in itself
Much less the boy back in the body
So, he accepts the blood at the altar

He knows love asks for all you have inside you

I left flesh in the keyboard this time

The hum of a fan stirring wisps the hairs end to end and I fear the click fuzz of the computer coming to life

VIII

The boy begets love and calls it women

The first time we kissed I was a hand full of 40 pages and two wrong clicks of the mouse
We are more than our understandings, but I have never learned how to be more than this
Plastic wrap coating of a snapshot confusion
I am not of my body and all that it wants
But her finger fishes the voice out and I am a silent bed of emptiness

We make (*fuck*) and call it 9 years
Much longer if I accept how it has changed me
We are what we eat they say, and my skin falls from bones and I smell of Robitussin

The hands have learned while I was asleep

And I am still trying to pick this love clean and flush my teeth till I can't taste anymore

IX

Some days I never left room 207 and Adele still plays through the receiver

I wish I had enough answers to be honest
But tomorrow is always a future we haven't lived yet
If time was a language, I was still learning to speak the past
Not understanding how to move a sentence forward

Sticks and stones may break our bones, but sickness lives inside me

X

Art imitates life, but if all paintings moved you would give them color.
She was old enough to make a history book of my body
But still asked where the scars came from

I have hidden the truth from myself long enough it has become bed sheets
And I am still wondering why I have nightmares
When all I don't want to believe
Sleeps with me in the night

A third of a century inscribed on my coffin
A man now
Or, fog that has called itself into existence
But these are all the loose teeth I bare in the corners of my palms

I am still the boy in the dresser
The stain lined paper mural of a shadow
I want to be enough for myself
And have enough of myself to love someone else
But I keep searching with my hands in the dark

I see only daffodils rotting under the leaves
A boyfriend of a full stomach making promises like grease to antacid
Heartburn and a sickness that runs the belly empty
My love asks for my name
And I let all my secrets run from an open spout
But the water muddles and thickens in the night

I am a festering of fingers crawling from my body
This is what I call love
A confused mess of scabs I scratch at in my childhood
A naked mess of flesh and mass that I try to stand up like a gentleman in my absence
I am as grotesque as my body makes me

XI

Forgiveness is a sound I whisper into my pillow every night I sleep next to you

She doesn't speak of the man that haunts the room when we are away
She makes lemonade of my lips and I learn to drink her kisses sour
It is a sweet crystal refracting everything I have been beneath the covers
And my body shivers in colors I have never known

I try to explain my body and all I have ever mistaken

She rests her eyes and asks me to hush
I am a small thing in a toy chest of memories

She looks at me as if everything she has ever said repeats:
"*I see you*"

My sins lament like water from my body
I am as soft as relaxation
I ease the delicate wings of demons from my back
They are a brittle kind of reality

And she repeats:
"*We are all a gathering of things we can't control from our past*"
"We are all human"
"Flawed but oh so alive"

THE SUN SETTING THE FIRST TIME

We were all children of the fields
Breaking our backs to let our arms sway to the wind
We were young once

That Saturday in May, I swear I saw the horizon form at the tips of their fingers
When they stretched their arms out east to west and said:
"tthhhiiiiiiis much"

I asked them if they loved me

Those were the simple times
When an ice-cream cone and some skittles could change the world

I suppose we all must learn loss at some point

Maybe that is why I met them
Broke my hands open like orchids
I thought I knew what love was
I thought I knew what the sun setting felt like

But you never truly do
Till you realize you can't get some days back
And you are left saying good morning to the darkness

I know how far the horizon reaches now
And if I could go back and tell myself
I would say:

It ain't that far
It ain't that far

TESTIMONY OF THE SUN

In the summer of '98
We ravaged the apple trees
For all they had
Broke the skin red and juice of our mouth
Full
Sour
Crushed and rotten stems hard as wood
We stumbled down Midway Ave
Scuffing up our knees
More than our shoes
Made a blood pact in
More ways than one
Juggled firecrackers
Till our hands burned
And our lungs caught enough smoke
We named it nicotine
For six days we stayed up all night
Devoured enough of the dark
We claimed we were vampires
Lived in the basement and became
The same monsters that called us
Into the cobwebs
Once when the lights flickered
And we told ghost stories
About our childhood
We licked our lips cleaning bones
From the soil

I still don't remember
Where we placed the daggers
We dug up from the backyard
I just remember everything we
Replaced them with came from our bodies
And how
We said we shouldn't be here
Alive
Living like we owned all the
Breaths we took
Chasing the deer through the trees
And rusting our hinges on dreams

We thought we were everything invincible
Steel and stones and everything
Our ancestors left behind
We were wrong
We were just children
Who hadn't learned how to bleed yet
Calling ashes snowflakes
In the summertime

WHEN A GUN BEGINS TO BE A GUN

After – Buddy Wakefield

When I joined choir, I was barely older than morning dew
Chased the rainbow of my father's voice refracting in the sun
I was good at catching violin strings left hanging like laundry
On a Sunday morning

Once
Before I realized what had happened
I let a horse loose in the brass section

The crackle of horns burst into life
And rumbled
The stands empty

Control doesn't come easy in my family

A few summers past sundown I got my first job answering phones
Spoke like I knew a thing about a thing
But it still never came easy

One day an angry customer came calling
And my father answered
The way he used to
Crawled up through my throat
Like I wasn't speaking

The past can startle you when it comes calling

After that day
I let out a hushed hymn that sounded like
Asking for a ceasefire

When I think back to the chorus
It repeated:

You may be blood, but not your father
Don't let him recite for you now

ROADKILL AND OTHER MYTHS

Some days when I look at myself, I am a deer in headlights
But what do you do when you start to resemble the car
A deer is not a vehicle, but don't they hit the same
Head on and reckless

My face
Resembling a 30-year-old car:
I have seen this body of a rusting heap before
Barreling down on my childhood

I called it anger
I called it burning wreck
I called the car *man*

I am not this car
This aggression
This metal body for breaking
                        I am the deer

But once you have been hurt by a weapon
You are afraid to become one
You will often see yourself reflected in their metallic
Replace your name with fear
Until your face resembles it

Adolescence can look like survival when
Mating season is a 4-year residency in growing up
Mark your territory like a rub is the only way to write your name

Kiss the gravel with your teeth enough
And you will forget what your own mouth is supposed to taste like

When I was a fawn
I ground the velvet off my antlers enough times to know
Masculinity was a weapon
I said it like windshield but wrote it down like destruction
On anywhere it would land
Even when it was me

And didn't you know

Boys can become bucks if you make them
So, call me young buck of a man
Accident in the forest   call me an accident

When you learn its definition like me
You walk into everything like it's a fight
Like this hasn't been a hunt you have been outrunning since birth
Like you don't have to look both ways before crossing the street
Call this kind of trust another word for pain
When you learn to move your mouth through the vibrations of a car
How do you begin to speak when you start to make the same rumbling sounds

I wish I knew masculinity through a different voice like
Can ambition be more than anger if you make your family sound like wilderness
Can you know sex without clothing yourself in pornography
Can you be a father if you never leave
Can you be more than violence
Be more than abuse
Be more than a weapon

Can you hold onto someone with antlers and never hurt them
Can you see the light on the road and not become the fear

Am I the deer or the car
Barreling down this road
Even if I find myself on a different path
Full throttle
Heart an engine that hasn't quit yet
With this loose muffler smile that hangs and scrapes sometimes
This flat tire speech that keeps speaking even when the rubber has worn off

It will sound like
(*It will sound like*)
I am not the car
I gotta keep running
I am not the car
I gotta outrun this
I am not the
I am not the

                                      Car

MAKE A MEAL OF THE SOFT

If you could break the skin, would you
Like a mother's cooking
Warmth is not a hand, but has it held you
Beat you raw like a butcher's cut
Till you are left watery in your bones
A wave breaks a child's smile down to remembering
Not all things that are gentle
Can be explained
I have lost this *word* in my manhood
The same way a forest can lose itself
In a book
Maybe we have all traveled this road too far
Run soft serve and hunger
Till our brain shivers at the thought
Of winter
Have our teeth of it
The manner our grandmothers did
Do you still feel how sweetness left you open
Rain spoke of you in silence
You are still left searching for the whispers in the willows
There are days you still try to cup your palms like flowers
I hope you too are lucky enough
To see a fist unravel itself into
Happiness
Trying to ask yourself where it went
It was hard to see my father cry the first time
We never spoke of it
Boys make such good dams of their bodies
Some words can make weeds of your vocal cords
We all want to be whole enough to be human
Tenderness is a small thing missing
In every meal
I want to serve myself

DAYDREAM ME A TOTO

I am a tired clustering of clouds
Still trying to look like my imagination
Trying to be swept up in a dust storm
Strong enough to get lost in

WHAT IS A CRACKED COFFEE CUP SUPPOSED TO HOLD

In the yard behind my apartment
I see a boy picking dandelions
He is so patient with his fingers
Not to ruffle the seeds loose from the stem
Such care set in eyes
What haven't they seen
But a flurry of wishes cast in the air

After he is gone
I return to the patch of weeds
My palms massive and disproportionate to the wild things
I try to pick one and it snaps and jostles about in the air

Where does a man go for wishes
When all his hands are shears
And all his dreams have left him

THE LAST CRY OF THE BUFFALO

They will say we walked this land with grace
But were too heavy to make it beautiful
They will say we were too wild to be free
But we were just an assortment of possibilities
Waiting to be taken
They will mention our fury first
But will never have graced our hide
Seen the softness that knots itself into our mother's quilts
Rested on the fields our hooves carved out of the land
They will never name us kings
As we are the last of the honeybees
They will hunt us down till the blood soaks the soil red
When we cry out and let our songs drift over the plains
They will say we went crazy
Ran off over the cliffs screaming
They will say our voices took the land with it
They will say we were all just animals

                                        Now just hauntings in the wind

WHEN THE FACE IS TOO MUCH TO WEAR

One of my favorite memories was going to the Barnum and Bailey's Circus. The wonders of the world sprawled out onto an arena floor like magic. My mother tells me she remembers a sad clown and how it scared me. My face mirrored the dropping sadness through my fingers. There was an odd sense of understanding.

These days I make broken glass of smiles
The solstice is only a half moon
Of big top stories and I think of how I pull
The coat hanger from my body
Make a ringmaster of my cheeks
So I can stand here again like a clown

It is an easy thing to smile
To masquerade
My own mouth and taste the feeding

To be in awe of
Whenever I'm enough
Whenever I'm lost in a snake's tongue
Long enough to run into the bright lights
Making good promises of my blood

That's what circuses do

Put the fleeting wilderness in a cage
Just to make a show of it
Everyone forgets the collar
Ears whistling to a good roar
This glitter light laugh that always gets a
Cannon shot applause

For a moment

They always say
The hardest things to see
Are right in front of you
And doesn't that sound like magic

We all have become such great performers

Turned contortionist
The lion that rests in all of us
It has managed to fit into our bodies
What a small place this has become
Living between smiles and laughter

Do you see the clown car
I have made of my mouth
I can fit so much melancholy
Without being asked where it goes

Do you ever stay long enough to see
The yellow hue of light turn cold
Until they tear down the tents
After the show

Do you stay to see the clown
After the makeup has come off
There is always so much humanity
Left to dirty the rag

And so many smiles left
Lining the floor

AIR

Hold your hand out to catch the air

We can believe in something
If we just feel it
If we let it reach down inside us
With open palms clawing at our empty bellies
Waiting for the rumbling retch

We can believe in something
If we just hear it
We have made a mockery of this invisibility
Like this breath wasn't given to us in the first place

I have turned my back to the wind
Because a storm has never told me something I didn't already know
About myself
Like a weathervane never spoke to the weather
And asked it too where it was headed
Just ask every person who has climbed my family tree
The paper it is written on is similarly
A metaphor for death

How hard it is to chase
This Midwestern wind
When somedays you are just a chain link
Fence trying to keep everything out

How hard it is to unravel your lungs
Peel them back like open faced fingers
Till you believe in your own breath again

Air does that
Makes you feel like you are never good at holding onto anything

Maybe this is not really about the wind
Maybe this is about a bouquet of flowers
I keep trying to grow out of my chest
I know we are all just trying
To taste the sun enough to
Grow out of the darkness

How often have you held your breath
Because you are too afraid that it will never return

I sometimes stand making
My hand a windflower weathervane
Searching for a delicate breath to catch

Letting the lungs blossom despite knowing
Something can suffocate you
Even if you never see it

HAIR CAUGHT IN THE DRAIN

I	welcome this like a good mourning
cut	the hair to a length that remembers
less	of who I was and who I am still
to be	is to have survived in this like a

***

The morning after is always a
Showerhead of thoughts
Closed eyes, the water, naked tile
How we must
Be vulnerable before we can be clean
Make a storm drain out of anything that
Hasn't taken from us yet
Retch the body till anew
Ask a hug from anything that will hold
The inside, inside
I have asked more of a wall than myself lately
I need to speak what the silence tells me
Learning how to walk on your own
Can look a lot like falling
Or moving on
Or sometimes a funeral procession
But you don't always need a six-foot hole
To make a grave of the past or
To break the ground anew

A WHISTLE IN THE TUB DRUMS

Today I will not speak of the overcast
My mind has pulled the dirt from my feet
Made a cave of me
I was the raw lamb in the wild
I have seen the hunger and how
The sun can pull the carnivorous
From your bones after sleeping
Build a tent of the day and tell you to remain
Forever seems as long as some moments
I have held hands with structures much sturdier than me
Support can often be a silent thing
The inner parts of me have left enough times to know
I am not much of a doctor
But who hasn't tried to swallow
A twelve pack of goodnights rest
Tried to keep anything down to feel full
I have made s'mores and sandwiches of
Worse things
Roasted my thoughts over matchsticks
And candle wicks
Some days I have made friends with the worms
All you need is a cold glass of a bad night
To make survival
Sound like you are trying
I have read enough books
To know how to make a campfire story of my body
But an act of courage can be as simple as
Another morning

BODY OF WATER

There was a river here once
Before the streets took its name
Before the steel sounds shoveled
The grit and asphalt through our bodies

Before the bodies

Some days you can see it
This river
Between the cracked concrete that has
Stolen so many floods from us
We no longer know what this land
Was supposed to look like

Some days I hear it
This river
When I suffocate the air with my ears
Make this overpass a conch shell
Turn this street corner a crested wave
That has held more water than me lately

I remember when I was a child
People would say:
"If you follow a river long enough it will lead anywhere"

Well I know I have walked the
Rivers back home long enough to know
A river is never long enough to find a home in yourself

I have made rivers of creek beds
Enough times to know what a body of water can become
To know all you need is some concrete
To wash over

You can make anything look like
A shoreline if you have
Enough blood in you

Maybe we were all supposed to meet here
Like scattered shells ground to sand

Turned bank of a rusty river that has
Always run red with clay

There is iron in the soil here
And some day they will find mine here too

Maybe you have chased the edge of this riverbed
Maybe you have found a destination
Made of lost street signs and promises
Felt this ground grip you
Like an open doorway as it urges you to
Come in

And you are
Standing at the edge of this intersection
This river of names receding your hope
Clutching the arms of midday sun like you
Are not ready to let go yet
The current of steel sounds
Urging you to make a bed of this earth

I too know how ankles can become cinderblocks
It is so hard to find the surface
When drowning sounds like an exit

When you clutch the wheel a little less
Close your eyes
Sink deep into your seat
And let the air carry you

I too have named death home
There are days I wish to reside there

Days I have felt like an antenna strapped to a car headed west going eighty
Chasing the sunset

But depression and suicide are easier to
Talk about in metaphors and **silence**
And
I have wanted to make a coffin
Of this car

But maybe

We paved over this crossroad for a reason
Or made a street of this river
So, we could take the long way
Home

ICARUS'S GREAT HELLO

We all speak to the night differently
Making conversations with our shadows
We all want to be important enough
To be remembered in the morning
To wake up inside ourselves
Trap our names with our mouths
Some days we must make a rainbow
Out of anything
Make a tornado look easy enough to wear
Some days we must speak of secrets
The ones that we keep with the ground
That feather the spine
Some days we must ask our teeth
To rattle louder than the windows
We all have a plastic-bottle-aluminum-can
A shaking hello that we ask to leave us
We have all made wings of our limbs
Broke bones with feathers and air
We are a heavy thing
A flightless bound that has
Made a thick wound
Of trying
But we survive
Into the night
We survive

THE NIGHT BARKS BACK

Snip the snarl leaving the claws where they tremble
There is no room for rumble and gnashing
Let the wild run out of you like a loose tongue
Smile; and breathe deep with your bones
Like the body hasn't experienced this attention before
Anxious is the power that calls the wicked out of you
Leave the blood on the canines this time
Do not fear the sound of your own voice
Face found in the oven of this heat
Speak with your teeth and let your fur stand for you
Even when you are tired
Let the meal leave you hungry
Don't give into this and all that rests behind the door
Leave it
And let it be what it's always been
Unknown
But try not to chase the footsteps that haunt the night
Try not to feel the rippling tide of muscle that
Calls your senses to lament
This can be an open window with a good breeze
If you lean into the glass
And let your eyes chase the things that escape in the trees

I DRINK THE MILK BECAUSE IT IS WHOLE

I grew up in the dairy state
Where an open field was as wide as the horizon
A pointillism of livestock and barns
Scattered like lost Legos on the ground

I'd almost say
I could build something here
Like the world seemed to one day open and
Anyone could just reach out and caress
The first flicker the sun coughed up into waking

I have been told that
"Drinking milk strengthens your bones"

The brittle I have become on the inside
I often imagine it like fingernails
A splintering mess of nerves
This itching breaking inside of me
I wish to chew off the ugly
From my frame
Pasteurize my anxious sour smiles
Till I resemble a clean thing

I drink the milk because it is whole

I consume to make
A better vessel of myself
A whole thing that I too wish I was
I try to fill the vacancy
Wish to trust the pasture of this
Skin and skeleton
Everyone is willing to devour
Anything as long as it makes them
Feel strong again

Here

We drink like the night
Turn our mouths inside out
Let the milky way define us

Here there are generations
Of farmer's hands
All pulling from the soil in unison
There is enough land for us all
To lay here one day

And some of us have
I have known enough raven's names that I find straw bales lining my chest
A hard breath and a chaser no longer
Burns them from my throat
A full glass can make anyone feel invincible
But no amount of milk can bring back the dead

I would know
I have turned enough wooden barrels into caskets to see my own shadow
Held the breath of a wheat field enough times to wake up holding a shovel

A grave is easier to dig
        When you don't remember doing it
                Everything is easier when you don't remember

I can tongue tie myself
Laugh my way out of pain
A blackout is just the night taking back
The milky way from our bones

Out here there is a farm every mile
The milk runs so cheap it lines our spines
Grows roots in our young like a lighthouse

How safe we can feel here
Chasing our family to the slaughter
Tradition has become
The milky white light
That leads us

FISHBOWL

Everything feels barren
When the bottle runs dry
When you are still left standing
Uncorked and vulnerable
Alcohol has never saved me
From myself
Much less others
But I have stood
One and three quarters in
Before
And I am still barely wading
How easily someone can pour into
An ocean but
Pouring the ocean out of yourself
Looks more like a dry landing
Message in the bottle
Over a bed of rocks named regret
All I have to show for it
Is a couple old faces and a
Crumpled piece of paper
This feels like leaving again
Surrounded by a last call
Empty pockets
A glass bottle with nothing left
But my reflection

THE BOY/THE BOTTLE/THE ERASURE

Erasure of the definition of Erasure, as defined by Poets.org

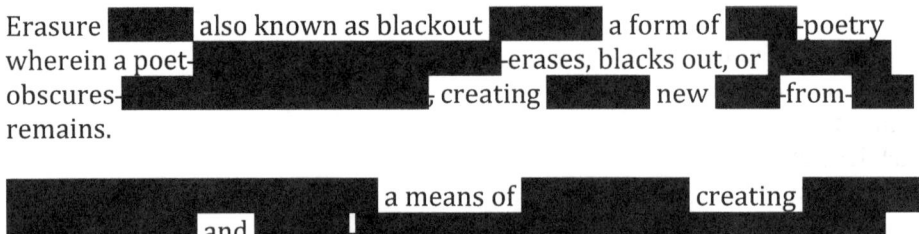

Erasure   also known as blackout   a form of   -poetry wherein a poet-   -erases, blacks out, or obscures-   , creating   new   -from- remains.

                         a means of   creating   and   of confrontation,   to   -existing

***

Self-medication like
A boy
Remembering
Skin

Pain
Editing
The worst out

An erasure

A line
When all that is original
Is gone

But what existed
Was never truly theirs
To keep

THERE ARE NO FOOTSTEPS IN THE DEEP END

We are all doctors making prescriptions of receipts

I never talk about what it is like to have a shadow. You are never ready to
be of your blood. Make a handful of promises and leave them.
When I was five, I learned I would be an older brother.
We never see the eyes that watch us the closest. This is all a dance we make
of our understandings. Choreograph the words and the way we speak them.

        I have made a medicine cabinet of the corner bar
        Swallowed the glass full and made a chaser of my smile
        It is easy to make a mockery of the face
        Till you rinse lavender with your blood
        I thought I was dealing happiness for smiles
        I thought a lot of things
        I've been the open tomato sauce can in the garbage
        Buried friendships in more ways than one
        Beneath time and dirt
        I have been the man walking without a light
        I have been the groundhog and the shadow
        Shaking hands with the snow

The night my parents drove three hours down to Whitewater
To see if my brother was alive
I realized hand-me-downs can be made
Of a life we used to wear
It can be a half empty night
Reemerged as the fool on the table
The swollen eye full on Fleischmann's
Or four knuckles, a steel rod
Anything that asks for more than you can offer
Anything that wakes you at 3am like a threaded needle

        I have made an apple orchard of bad decisions
        Picked the land clean and sipped on misery

        I tell myself you are not the wicker basket
        I tell myself you are not the silver glass reflection
        You are the light I now walk into
        I tell myself lies
        I tell myself you will be alright

You are not the darkness I leave behind
You are the future I walk into

SAP AND SAPLINGS

The men in my family
Were all born like matchsticks
Burning through time
A wilting combustion of soiled timber
All shaved down from the same rotten oak

One year, they milked the maple trees of all they had
Filled each bucket like a blood bag
The sap ran so dirty it became mud
Overfilling into their hands
They say the roots curled and buckled
Reached up out of the earth
Claiming each of their children

When my grandfather died, they produced a will like heritage
Named it stroke
Named it heart attack
Soaked the pages till their hearts wept
A thick poisonous sap that
Seized all their arteries
Signed it with a yellowish wax

I have been given this land just as my father
And his father
All the men that tried to grow here
Like little saplings
Born into a fire
Veins popping and jittery
So alive with death
A curse
A blade that was born in our chests
Flowering needles
Petals of blood

When my father found out he had cancer
I wondered what rot has nestled and fed
The roots I lay as I walk
What sludge has marinated my bones

People wonder why we act so feverishly

A tireless bunch of stubborn Germans
Like we were handed a clock at birth
And were asked not to let it tell time

SANS

It is January and the snow has come
Consumed the ground and everything with it
You learn to live with passing
In time and person
Learn that winter is a cold thing
Bites and means to use the teeth

Funerals never get easier
You just learn to dress better for them
Learn to sculpt the snow with your arms
Till you make wings of the ash
We all wish to become angels
And leave our mark on the untouched

I lay in the snow and become it
The hush of the dead laments in the open
I say goodnight to everything that hasn't slept
The darkness moves before the sun
And I with it

THESIS ON THE FEELING OF WINGS

When mom told me you had cancer, I laughed, or joked, or let out a still frame of my life that keeps ringing-
I am not sure reality ever caught my lungs. Wrestled understanding back down inside of me, or if I have been chasing yesterday all these years.
The day they cut you open like your brother, I still thought
                                                                      you could fight it off.
I guess I am still learning that being a man doesn't always look like fighting
                             but sometimes it does.
Sometimes removing a part of yourself can look like a balled-up fist, or maybe that is all I remember of my hands that day

                                      ***

It was the year I returned to the snow
And all the Christmas gifts were made of curses
It was the year your heart fluttered, till it didn't
The year I broke the silence of birthday wishes and asked you
                                                                           "just try"

I can see how recovery sounds a lot more difficult
Being brought back to a body that has already rejected you

But who else will play the role of my father?

Fighting isn't always done with fists
Sometimes the fight has to be done for you
I have given you all the secrets I have known of trying

Most mornings now, I wake up with feathers caught in my hair from learning to love the sun, or
How to carry all this. I still wonder if we could have arrived here otherwise.
When we talk now, I see yesterday as it is today

Healthy

Maybe this is what the bird feels learning to fly:
I remember watching you and thinking anything was possible

                                    now I know it is

A GOOD DAY'S WORK

It was the year the willows didn't sway, and the barn filled with wasps
Till the air hummed and hissed out a slow sizzle in the Wisconsin summer

All the wood rattled with nuts and bolts till they loosened from rot

That year my father put away his white sneakers
That had grown green with grass

Taught me how to use the tractor
and ride a horse till I sketched links and wire in my skin

That summer we dug a sweat out of our pores with shovels
Till we littered the field with fence posts

Hands blistered up burns that stayed longer than the sun
Longer than words, or stains, or the things that broke them

I don't know why I remember digging those holes with him
But work was something closely tied to who my father was

A day was as long as it needed to be
To get the job done

But it wasn't work that reminded me of this
The time we bled and lost skin together

Till the sun was swallowed by the sky
And mom's cooking called us in

In this moment
we built something together

It doesn't sound like much, digging some fence holes
But you tend to get into things when you open up the earth enough

Dug so deep our words covered our hands truthful
And all the land we grew from broke and crumbled beneath us

There is a lot that can be said by the shovelful
So much so that you can forget why you are digging

Why you ever started in the first place
Putting up one fence post at a time

You start to wonder why you ever started separating it
Ever let the metal bite the skin and grass till it made a mess of it all

Why you called them walls
And hid behind them

That summer we learned more than what a good day's work can bring
We learned how much time we missed

And how much we cherished it
When it returned

A MILLIONAIRE / A TAXI DRIVER / A TAX PAID

I have seen a man shave a dream down to a dollar
Make a million sense of pocket change
He wore smiles like he lived
And he has
All he needed was a person or
Good company

A display case of oddities and travels
Spoke more languages than actually spoken
Especially when fixing just about anything
                                      Fuck/Shit/Bitchin' thing/God damn it
A proper mouth has seaworthy sails
And his tongue was a Marine

2008 was a rough five years
Learned a degree and hard work can lose you a home

You know:
                They say you can be anything when you grow up
                  Ask you to condense yourself down to success
                  Find someone who is dumb enough to say you are
                            Be enough to believe it
              I have seen what a man with three diplomas can do
                    I have seen how heavy pride can be

                                                                           You know:

    Taxi drivers and journalists meet the same amount of interesting people
            Ask the same amount of interesting questions

I have heard more stories carved into the back seat of cars and bathroom
                                              stalls
        Learned that some pieces of paper are worth more than others
           But what message carved in a trunk has ever graced a resume

I have seen a man chase a million dollars
Enough times to make losing look successful
He doesn't smile much anymore
All he ever needed was a person
To tell him it is alright to fall

Spruce trees do it all the time
Look what wonderful stories
They become

THE POCKET KNIFE THAT LEARNED TO WHITTLE FLUTES

If I was a feature of my father
I would be his mouth
Full
An unwavering gritty mass
Of happiness
Sweaty pores contracting and pulled together
A showcase of resolve
Clenched teeth gleaming like trophies

He has a practiced way of turning a heavy sigh into a word like reasonable

He is never bad, broken, blood drenched and ruined
All the things he has burdened with unyielding strength

The same intensity it has taken for him to become the greatest man I have ever known
Makes more than a good thing out of the worst days
And there were a lot of "worst" days

But what person hasn't bit through a few lips
Trying to make a smile out of a broken thumb
An empty wallet
And hunger

What bird hasn't thrown up a few times to feed their young
Made themselves sick of a good thing
Trying to consume all that this barren land has to offer

What are teeth for, if not to chew

Through the hard cud of this tundra
The mashing of consumption
Of life
To get everything from this earth that our bodies can

What are we if not
The boundless unraveling of history
Kept in blood
Of our fathers' and theirs'
An ancestral conversation

Of chewing mouths all swallowing at once

What am I if not of my father and his
The will of a German man
Stubborn but strong

I speak like fingers tilling the earth out of my cheeks
Like Iowa
A field of bladed stalks
A loose barn door with a country creak
Rusted from staying in the same spot too long

All the skin that has shriveled and returned back to the ground
The organs that make flutes of the earth worms
There is so much sound in this body
Turning us into wind chimes
The same way our hands turning the ground made the birds sing
And our bellies full

And it is that same voice that stays with me now
2,000 miles from the closest thing that sounds like home
But I own it
Like a hard cider that bites the tip of your tongue stupid
Or a hard drink that stiffens your chin like starch on a new suit
I learned how to take both down smiling

Because we were all born of clay and dust
We all moved like the water our roots laid in
Wild enough to never be of any other kind
But strong enough we named it free

If I was a feature of my father
I would be his lungs
His voice
And all the songs they have claimed
In that blue car we road in just long enough to fish out a few melodies

Or even now
when the air is too free to be worked and all that grows from it is laughter
In the early winter of Florida
Where nothing has died but the sickness
Where we all have become open mouths of dancing teeth
Moving to the sounds of music

CLEANED

I make order of the frogs that chirp and hum away the sound of the pour. The tap and croak choke that makes a love of the air. It is an open window and I am the home. The body. The inner space that breaks the scent of leaves rotting in the crisp cold. The bite, the cape, the drape, the nape, the neck, the whole mess.
The shutter clips a memory:

> *Bed, white pillows and a shiver that holds the body down.*
> *My ears collecting rainwater to drown in the calm of the fall.*
> *Crack the wicks of door jams and candle flames.*

[This will be the last time]

Made rusted hands of my feet
They grip the carpet and I am alone
Scissor fingers of a doorknob
I cut the infected from the stomach of this
The I and I alone

> I left myself in that apartment
> We all make homes of the easy
> But pain is a slow drug
> And it has drug me from my own

I look back at the stale forms. Everything looks clean from the outside. Everything always did. Some fruit make mash and hastened pulp of the interior. They make a shower's cold release of me. In the beginning I was a useless thing. Only of the jaw. A chewed wad of thoughts she made of me.

> In the evenings I am the boy again.
> The he, the she, the gravity
> It pulls the weight out of you
> And I am left chasing the same pain from different names

[Mind over matter, don't mind the matter over mine]
A good lie
Tender the steak you make of me
        [The last meal of an empty plate]

The paint that dried on the floor
Removed the carpet
Made a hardwood floor of me
           [Words and knuckles, the same marks under skin]
Blank, faceless, the end after a long beginning
All the hot air that has left this place
Break off from this good winter, and leave
                [I am love and this is not of the body]
I am free

DISCOVERY

Off beyond the hawthorns
In a city of old rusting relics that couldn't quite find
What they were supposed to be if ever found
I stowed away a chestnut in an old refrigerator
Birthed from a 74' Ford pickup and box springs
That coiled like vines from the earth

The seed I planted there in the trash bled for six days after leaving
Till the roots wrestled my heartbeat into oxygen
Grew out a system from forgotten decay
There are days I still don't believe in love
Or loving myself enough to love another
There is a shovel's deep worth discovering
That some things aren't meant for us all

I know I can be more than what is found there
Between the red berry trees
With old beds soiled and stained
Blood that litters the ground dark
And a fort I made of discarded things

There is more to me than what I buried here beyond the thorns
There is a trust that still hiccups at the sight of freedom
That musters the bile back down with a smile
I can't let the fear out of the fog

But I know where it keeps
I know where the film has peeled away from the whole
The orange rind that zests the taste buds back to life
I feel it every time it is broken open with an outstretched hand
Asking me to come

THE ILLNESS THAT WE BREED

When I met you
I was just as broken as I will ever be
A menagerie I keep to myself

I have taken this as far as it will ever go
By now I should have assumed what my name means
But some omens god keeps to himself

I wonder if you can ever love a half-made work of art
One who's framing is a little off
And the picture will never be understood

I wonder if I will be enough to look at
After the hot wax has evaporated, burned off,
And the light turns dim

I have met more than enough people
Who deemed me not enough
But don't imperfections build character

What if perfection was as good as you made it
Cause I have been working on myself for some time
And I am still not finished

But right now
I am a coffee spilt stained napkin hanging on the edge of a table in the Louvre
Just trying to make myself sound worthy of being seen

And you are
Every person that has ever stopped to look through this gallery
And thought I was truly art

THE NIGHT IS MADE OF LAUGHTER

Last night we had sushi again
Broke open our mouths with a
car ride that lasted long enough
to find ourselves in the dead of
night. There is no flavor for love
but I think I have been tasting it
every night we rolled tuna
between our tongues till our
smiles were kisses draped over
our bodies. You can find
friends here. Laughter shaking
the stools and a good
Mojito
We chased the future slowly.
Like arriving home at 2am didn't
matter. As if that night we
ran the sickness out of us.
Last night we stole back time
became rich off ourselves.
This life can be so beautiful
Running through the shadows.
All you need is a soft thing to
clench your teeth with.
To realize
The tender moments these are.

GINGERBREAD

Crack the shell
And feed the yolk to the mixing
Find a soft thing and keep the young
Blood is not a batter
But it likes to get into things
Molasses will stick and you will
Know your fingers dirty
Vanilla is a sweet thing to keep in the cupboard
Hide the good till they are ready
Knead the skin and the pain of history
Make a good dough of this
Hold the bowl and all that comes with it
Some will not like the taste
Find the spices between a loose jaw and a hard smile
Family does not always make a table of the warm
Know the brown
The burnt
The parts most will fear of the oven
Show them the flavor of a cooked thing
Even if they will not eat
Chew through the hard
Lose a tooth to the process
Lose more if the recipe asks it
You may find alone in this
Know that not all ginger and cinnamon
Taste the same

ASPHYXIATION OF PAIN

You make a quest of your bones
Lay the sleep beside you
Have you given the word to the rocks
Lapped the blood up with your having

Beauty has stolen the best
From us

You are a dizzying mess of smiles
An ink quill the night has written with
Hands
Feet
Tortured limbs that sway in the heat

We are a careless bunch of anxious
A storm of shadows draped over a façade
I have learned to love your pain
Make a hug of soft welcoming
Let the skin drown you in conversation
Or leave you at peace as the sun does

We have made a treaty of our lips
To make love through much less
Than our bodies can offer
I hold each word that breaks the rules
We have made hard candy of this
We have tethered our blood to
The earth
Made a church of this good worship
Held hands with the silence of ours
And hours alone

There is a night to remember here
A night to build of the couches and beds
I feel lungs in the darkness
The hot air grasping our insides
We can make anything of the shadows

I will hold you
Make weight of light and sound

Make anything of this

We can asphyxiate our wanting
Like love is still a selfless tradition

NEEDLES

She is the morning before the sun
Half-awake and full of eyes
She has never birthed a full night's rest
Just toiled tomorrow into existence
Held hands with the moon till
The moon got tired

She knows the night like an old shirt
Wears it like a loose fitting
She has never asked for this
Troubled power itch of thought
She makes a holy burial of dreams
We all wish we could see the things
That talk to us at midnight
And she has

Strength is no more a physical act
As it is a battle with the senses
She spins the earth with her smile
The world has made nails of the soil
And she has learned to make a
Dancefloor of pain

TRUTH IS A GHOST OF OUR SPEECH

Last night we shattered the air into truth
And I have never unraveled my skin
Enough to fear the under
Enough to see the
/Apparition/
How long I have been a product of my
Thoughts. Of my unclean hands.
Have you ever held love
It is a delicate wild of thorns
We all want to chase after this pain
Make a garden of everything we know
But we are all untamed and edgeless
Trying to make a sensible thing of this
/Love/
An unseen field of butterflies
We all try to touch the future
Without expecting it to change
I have made a fool of my heart
Broke pain open like a selfish bottle
Held a bounding main in my lungs and refused
To drown
I too have admitted, wrong.
Held a cherry from the broken branches
I have asked everything of the wild
That the wild will ask of me
/Pain/
A rose that gave itself up to love
Death has taken more than life from us
Sometimes we make
An orchard of our bodies
Only to have our hands pick the juice from
Our fingers
Only in the hush of palms
Have we made a good thing of the body
Loosened ourselves to another like
Stones in a river
/Words/
All we have in a storm of eyes, lips,
Blank faced and restless
We open our mouths to the new

Communication has made
A eulogy of our understandings
We often forget to make
Blossoms of our ears
Make bones of our confusion
My hands have lied to me
Made a love of the soft till it hardened
I need to learn to make
Tulips of my speech
/Again/

LUCID

A story is just a collection of dead trees that
We never let the earth keep
But what good is rich soil when we're poor
On loving our dirty hands

> *We had enough for the children we hadn't had*
> *In the mornings we never shared the covers*
> *Never let the cold bite us before the dawn shook our eyes open*
> *We never knew a splinter of a frame*
> *Just little words nestled between box springs and backboards*
> *That kept us up all night*

I keep finding us under my fingernails
A cold bed side and rustled covers
I should have slept in

The morning isn't anything but a full throat
Too dry to recite our dreams
Or a barren meadow we keep trying
to yield conversations of the night from

But sometimes it is a pair of eyes
That haven't woken up yet
A fearful breath on the downward whirl
Of a rollercoaster

Life is just as hard to live as it is to love and
Sometimes life is a percussion of atoms
Colliding in a crescendo of mathematical chaos

And sometimes it is us
    Joinery is just the act of marrying two pieces of wood

That is what I would say if I knew how to ask you

    We are just a collection of stories that
    Haven't found our way back to the ground yet

ODE TO THE MAN I AM TODAY

      If I shave, the razor will be sharp enough to cut the past from my body this time. Make a clean face of all my bad decisions till I can look at myself in the mirror again. I have learned to make tattoos of my scars. An art piece for the truth that is overcoming. There are so many impossibilities to make possible if you breathe them in. If you exhale expectations till your body remembers promise. There is no road to follow here: just dirty hands, feet, and a lot of blood I left behind.
I have learned to love painting the ground with failures again. Learned to let my heart speak for when my throat is full of ears. It is so easy to say the things you want to hear, but harder to live out the ones you don't. I have made a bed of forgiveness, even when I do not sleep in it. On the worst days when the lights dim enough to make the night rest inside of me, I have learned that some birds sing at 3:00 am. The world can sound like an orchestra in autumn or just the falling of acorns. Silence is as beautiful as it needs to be, and I have learned to make my bed with a sheet set of insomnia. I no longer need to pull the blinds on my eyelids with bottle caps. These days I rest with a heartbeat that is more restless than mine. I drank down love in a bar and have been hung over heels for her ever since. I have learned to make things with my hands again, even when I am afraid, they will be too fragile to hold on to. I have learned to be fragile. Patience is something I still wait for on occasion. But some things are just not worth waiting for. Sometimes the sky cracks the clouds open long enough to think the weather mastered perfection. Other times it is just her smile. Luck is not something I would gamble on, but I would make a full house out of this. With nothing to lose but everything. I can only be all that has made me. Two tired hands and a dream for something more.

DARE TO BE

If we let the past
It would run time like leaves
Make maple of our blood and
Stir our nostrils wild
Pancakes and good jazz on Sunday morning
We would be like we were always meant to

This is an ode to you
And us
To all the people who ever laughed louder than the sky
Who made hopscotch of puddles
This is for the dreamers that still converse with the night
For the ones who make a home out of anything
For the treetop in all of us that still reaches for the sun
Let's make a miracle sound like our own again
Reimagine the things we made of the clouds
Then dare to do it all again

ACKNOWLEDGMENTS

Thank you, Three Mile Harbor Press. You all saw something in my writing that for a long time I did not see in myself. Your patience, dedication, and willingness to take chances has given my voice a place to live. Thank you, Paul Genega, and Pamela Hughes for allowing me to take this journey with you.

Thank you to the Orlando poetry, slam, spoken word, and writing community at large. Thank you to the friends, teammates, coaches, hosts, editors, and competitors I have met along the way. Thank you to the people who gave me a space to perform, write, and learn. Thank you to everyone who has ever graced me with your words, and the other endless people who have helped give me the courage to breathe mine into existence. Thank you to the numerous venues, coffee shops, stages, and spaces, that helped foster this inside of me.

Thank you, Joy Stokes. Without your guiding hand, and encouragement this book would have never been possible. Your endless support, love, and fortitude has gone a long way in shaping my development as a writer and a person. Thank you for the edits, considerations, and endless critiques that have helped to cement my heart in this book.

Thank you to my family. To my mom, for always showing me that love is a strength all its own. I still don't know how you manage to make everything look so graceful. To my dad, who has shown me the will of living, and of becoming. You're an inspiration to overcoming, and second chances. I continue to look up to you, and your unceasing knowledge. Thank you both for the good and the bad and everything in between. To my brother, who has always believed in me even when I didn't believe in myself. For the drunken rants and pep talks you give at 3 AM. You are all wonderful, and a constant inspiration. Your collective well of love, and hard truths will always be with me.

Thank you to my friends, and random acquaintances who have helped stir these conversations inside of me. To the ones who have always been an open ear. Thank you all for listening to my stories, ideas, and incessant ramblings.

An earnest thank you to the editor of Narrative Northeast where the following poems were originally published: "Störrisch," "The Night Barks Back," "Moving On," "Lucid," "Ode to the Man I Am Today," and "Dare to Be."